Penguin Readers

THE EXTRAORDINARY LIFE OF ANNE FRANK

KATE SCOTT

LEVEL 2

ADAPTED BY HANNAH FISH
ILLUSTRATED BY ANKE REGA
SERIES EDITOR: SORREL PITTS

Some of the quotes in this book have been simplified
for learners of English as a foreign language.

PENGUIN BOOKS

UK | USA | Canada | Ireland | Australia
India | New Zealand | South Africa

Penguin Books is part of the Penguin Random House group of companies
whose addresses can be found at global.penguinrandomhouse.com.

www.penguin.co.uk   www.puffin.co.uk   www.ladybird.co.uk

Penguin Random House UK

The Extraordinary Life of Anne Frank first published by Puffin Books, 2019
This Penguin Readers edition published by Penguin Books Ltd, 2021
001

Original text written by Kate Scott
Text for Penguin Readers edition adapted by Hannah Fish
Text copyright © Kate Scott, 2019
Illustrated by Anke Rega
Additional illustrations pages 5 & 19 by Alice Negri
All illustrations copyright © Anke Rega, 2019, except pages 5 and 19 copyright © Penguin Books Ltd, 2021
Cover image copyright © Anke Rega 2019

The moral right of the original author and the original illustrator has been asserted

Printed and bound in Great Britain by Clays Ltd, Elcograf S.p.A.

The authorized representative in the EEA is Penguin Random House Ireland,
Morrison Chambers, 32 Nassau Street, Dublin D02 YH68

A CIP catalogue record for this book is available from the British Library

ISBN: 978–0–241–49311–3

All correspondence to:
Penguin Books
Penguin Random House Children's
One Embassy Gardens, 8 Viaduct Gardens,
London SW11 7BW

MIX
Paper from
responsible sources
FSC® C018179

Penguin Random House is committed to a
sustainable future for our business, our readers
and our planet. This book is made from Forest
Stewardship Council® certified paper.

Contents

People in the book	4
New words	5
Note about the book	6
Before-reading questions	6
Chapter One – Who was Anne Frank?	7
Chapter Two – Anne's early life	13
Chapter Three – Life in Amsterdam	16
Chapter Four – The secret rooms	20
Chapter Five – Life in the secret rooms	32
Chapter Six – The Nazis find the secret rooms	44
Chapter Seven – Anne's diary	48
Timeline	52
During-reading questions	56
After-reading questions	57
Exercises	58
Project work	62
Glossary	63

People in the book

Anne Frank

Otto Frank
(Anne's father)

Edith Frank
(Anne's mother)

Margot Frank
(Anne's sister)

Adolf Hitler

New words

argument

diary

exam

hide

win

Note about the book

Anne Frank lived in Germany. Adolf Hitler and the **Nazis*** **became** the **government** of Germany in 1933. In 1939, Hitler and the Nazis **invaded** Poland. This started the **Second World War** (WWII). The Nazis invaded many countries and took **control** of them. They sent the **Jews** from these countries to **camps**, and many of them died there.

The Second World War started in September 1939, and the end of the war in Europe was in May 1945. The Nazis killed more than six **million** Jews in the war.

Before-reading questions

1 Look at the title and cover of this book. What do you know about Anne Frank?
2 What do you know about the Second World War?
3 Read the back cover and the "Note about the book". What more do you know now?
4 What information would you like to find out from this book?
5 Do you have a diary? What do you write about in your diary?

*Defnitions of words in **bold** can be found in the glossary on pages 63–64.

CHAPTER ONE
Who was Anne Frank?

Anne Frank was a normal young girl. She was an intelligent child, and she was very good at writing stories. At a young age, Anne's **life became** very difficult. But Anne was **brave**, and she always smiled and laughed.

In the **Second World War**, Anne and her family had to hide from the **Nazis**. The Nazis wanted to kill **Jews**, and the Franks were Jews. The Frank family hid from the Nazis in **secret** rooms for more than two years. In the secret rooms, Anne wrote a diary. She wrote everything in it. She wrote about her life in the secret rooms and the people she was with. She also wrote about her **feelings**.

Anne's diary is now very famous all over the world. Many people read it, and it is a very **interesting** but very sad book.

At the age of fifteen, Anne died. Today, she is very famous. People across the world know her name and her face because of her wonderful writing.

Anne wrote a diary.

The Second World War started in September 1939.

Three years later, Anne and her family had to hide from the Nazis with some other **Jewish** people in secret rooms. Not many people knew about the Frank family and the secret rooms, but some people helped them. These "helpers" brought food and water to Anne and her family. This was very **dangerous** for the helpers, but they wanted to help the Franks.

Anne and her family

Someone told the Nazis about Anne and her family, and, on 4th August 1944, the Nazis found the secret rooms. The Nazis took eight people out of the secret rooms. In the next year, seven of those people died. Only Anne's father, Otto Frank, saw the end of the war and became an old man.

After the war, one of the Franks' helpers gave Otto Anne's diary, and he read it. Anne's writing was wonderful. Otto showed it to his friends, and he showed it to people in his family. Otto wanted everyone to read Anne's diary. He wanted them to read Anne's words about the war. Otto Frank saw his daughter's diary become famous all over the world.

Otto with Anne's diary

Anne's diary tells us about the lives of Jewish people in the Second World War. It tells of a difficult life for Jews and a difficult life for Anne and her family. But the diary also shows us Anne. It shows a brave, funny and kind young girl. Anne liked to talk a lot, and many people called her a chatterbox. But her diary shows us a kind girl. Anne thought about other people, and her diary showed this. Anne's diary became her best friend. She told it everything about her life and her feelings.

Anne wrote about the war.

Anne Frank's diary is very important. It tells us about daily life for Jewish people in the war. It was difficult for them to get food, and people were very **cruel** to them.

Anne was a normal young woman, and her writing is intelligent and interesting. Many years after she died, Anne's diary shows us a brave and wonderful girl.

But let's go back to the start of Anne's life . . .

CHAPTER TWO
Anne's early life

Anne Frank came into this world on 12th June 1929 in Frankfurt am Main in Germany. She had an older sister called Margot. Anne and her family were Jewish, and there were many other Jewish people in Frankfurt.

Baby Anne with her older sister, Margot

In January 1933, Anne was three years old. Adolf Hitler and the Nazis took **control** of Germany. The country now had a Nazi **government**, and life for Jewish people changed very quickly. "You must not use Jewish **businesses**," Hitler told non-Jewish German people. His government made many new **rules**. These rules were bad for Jewish people, and life became very difficult for them.

"German people are better than Jewish people," the Nazis said. "German people are more important than Jewish people, too."

Life became more and more dangerous for Jews. In the war, the Nazis killed **millions** of Jewish people in Germany and in other countries.

Adolf Hitler

Life in Nazi Germany was too dangerous for Anne and her family, and they went to Amsterdam in the Netherlands. They were happy in Amsterdam for six years, but then life changed again.

ANNE'S EARLY LIFE

On 1st September 1939, the Nazis **invaded** Poland, and the Second World War started. Countries from all over the world fought in the war. Great Britain, France, the United States of America (USA) and the Soviet Union fought together, but Italy and Japan helped the Germans. The countries fighting Germany were called the Allies.

The war started on 1st September 1939 and finished on 2nd September 1945 – six years of fighting. The Allies won the war, but the Nazis killed six million Jews in these years.

CHAPTER THREE
Life in Amsterdam

Anne and her family went to the Netherlands in early 1934. For about six years, things went well and they lived a normal life. Anne's father started his own business. Her mother, Edith, stayed at home, and she cooked and cleaned for the family. They were happy, and Anne had a cat called Moortje. Margot and Anne went to school, and they had a lot of friends there. They played sport with their friends after school, and they ate ice cream. The sisters learned Dutch – the language of the Netherlands. They could speak and write in Dutch. Anne was young, and she learned the new language quickly.

Anne and Margot went to school in Amsterdam.

Anne had her thirteenth birthday in Amsterdam. Her family gave her many things. She got flowers, clothes, a book – and a diary.

Anne loved her diary. It was her best friend, and she gave it a name – Kitty. She wrote "Dearest Kitty" at the start of every page. Many years later, "Kitty" (*The Diary of a Young Girl*) became a very important book for millions of people all over the world.

> "I hope to tell you everything.
> I don't tell anyone my true feelings,
> but I want to tell you.
> I hope for you to be my friend and to help me."

The first pages of Anne's diary were about her life in Amsterdam and all her friends. She liked some of her friends very much, but she did not like some other people. Anne did not show her diary to anyone. She could write anything, and she did not always write nice things!

Anne and her family lived in Amsterdam because Germany was dangerous for them. But, in 1940, Adolf Hitler and the Nazis invaded the Netherlands, and Hitler took control of the country.

The Nazis invaded the Netherlands.

Anne's mother and father were frightened. Life quickly became dangerous for Jewish people. Her parents had to make a plan – they had to hide from the Nazis. This was a secret plan, and they did not tell Anne and Margot about it until later.

Anne's diary tells us about this new life for Jewish people in Amsterdam.

Jews had to wear a yellow star;

Jews could not have a bicycle;

Jews could not use trams

or travel in cars;

Jews could only go shopping between 3 p.m. and 5 p.m.;

Jews could not go out of their homes between 8 p.m. and 6 a.m.;

Jews could not go to the cinema or many other places.

CHAPTER FOUR
The secret rooms

Today, many school children **worry** about exams. At school in the 1940s, Anne and her friends worried about exams, too. Anne was intelligent, but she did not always do well at exams. But Anne's mother and father did not worry too much about that. They only wanted Anne to be happy. Some of Anne's friends' parents worried about exams a lot, and Anne was very happy to have her parents. She wrote this in her diary.

Anne with her school friends

THE SECRET ROOMS

Anne talked a lot in class.

Anne talked a lot in class, and it made her teacher angry. One day, he told her to write a story called "A Chatterbox". Then he told her to write a story called "'Quack, quack, quack,' said Miss Chatterbox". Anne wrote a wonderful and funny story, and her teacher really liked it. Now, Anne could talk in class, and she did not have to write any more chatterbox stories.

Quack, quack, quack

But, on 5th July 1942, everything changed for the Frank family. Anne's sister, Margot, got a letter from the Nazi government. She had to go to a Nazi work **camp**. Many other Jewish people had to go to work camps, too, and it was very dangerous. The Nazis took Jewish men, women and children to work in the camps, and they had to work very hard. They only gave them a little bit of food and water, and they had to live in dirty rooms with a lot of other people. Many of the people in work camps became **ill** and died.

The Nazis also took Jewish people to other camps. In these camps, the Nazis killed many Jews.

A Nazi camp

Otto and Edith Frank now had a plan to hide from the Nazis. The plan was not ready, but Margot's letter changed everything. Otto and Edith did not want Margot to go to a work camp. It was too dangerous, and they wanted to hide their family from Hitler and the Nazis. Margot got her letter, and the next day the family went to the secret rooms. They could not take very much with them, and they had to leave a lot of their things at home. But Anne was very brave. "I remember many things, and these things are much more important than dresses," she wrote.

The family got ready for the secret rooms.

The family hid in Otto Frank's office building. There were many rooms and offices in the building, and, at the back, right at the top, there were the secret rooms. Anne and her family stayed in these secret rooms with the offices below. They had to be very quiet because they did not want people to hear them. The Franks built a bookcase over the door to the secret rooms. Now, no one could see the door or find the people in the secret rooms.

The Franks built a bookcase over the door.

There were four more Jewish people in the secret rooms with the Franks – a family of three and a man. The family were: Hermann, Auguste, and Peter van Pels. In Anne's diary, she calls them the van Daans. And the man was Fritz Pfeffer. In Anne's diary, she calls him Mr Dussel.

Anne had a bedroom with Mr Dussel.

Anne put pictures of famous people on the walls of her bedroom in the secret rooms. Otto brought the pictures for her from home. Today, you can see Anne's pictures on the walls of her bedroom. More than one person slept in each bedroom, and there was only one toilet for them all to use. Anne had a bedroom with Mr Dussel, and Margot had a bedroom with Otto and Edith Frank. The van Daans' bedroom was also the kitchen.

People worked in the offices all day, and the people in the secret rooms had to be very quiet. Then the office workers went home. Sometimes, Anne and the group went down into the offices below at night and listened to the radio. But, later, it became too dangerous to go into the offices, and they stayed up in the secret rooms all day and all night.

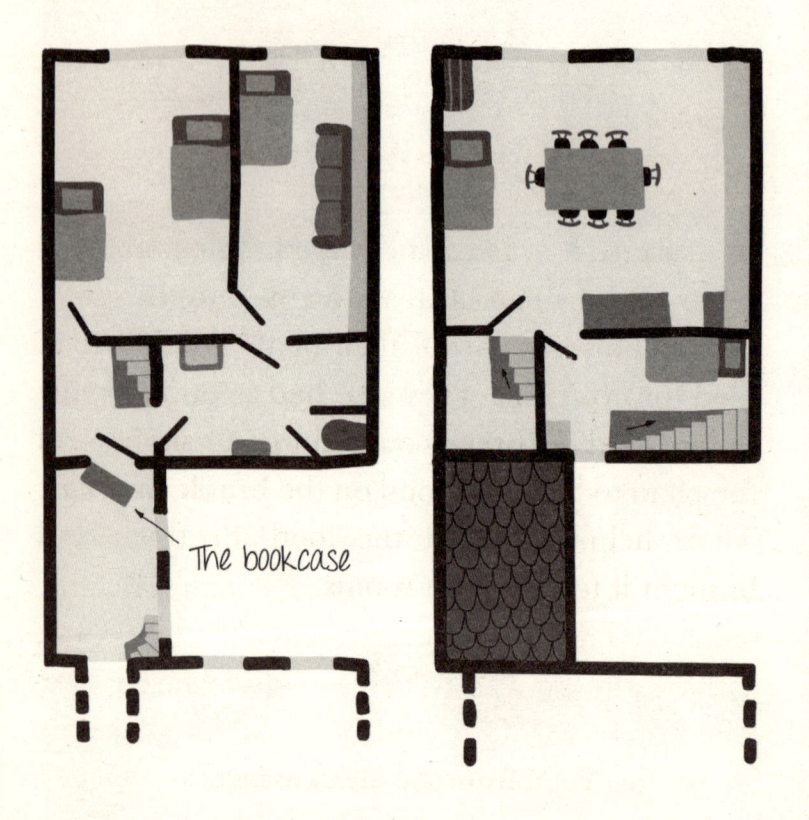

The bookcase

For two years, Anne, her family, and the other people in the secret rooms did not leave the office building. They could open a window but only at night. In the day, the windows were closed, and the secret rooms were dark and hot.

The kitchen in the secret rooms

At the start, they had a lot of food. Otto and Edith Frank and the van Daans brought it to the secret rooms. This was part of their plan, and they took food for everyone. They also had a lot of money to buy food. But they could not go to shops, and they had to buy their food on the **black market**. Their helpers bought the food for them and brought it to the secret rooms.

Food from the black market

But it became more and more difficult for the people in the secret rooms to get food. Some of their food became too old, and they could not eat it. And food on the black market became more and more expensive. Anne and her family often had to eat the same food again and again. Some food they did not like, and some food was old. Eating it was difficult, but they had to. Anne wrote about this in her diary, and she was always very funny.

Anne wrote funny things about food in her diary.

Two years is a long time for eight people to live together in small rooms. Sometimes, people had arguments, and Anne wrote about these arguments in her diary. Sometimes, at breakfast, lunch or dinner, no one spoke, and they all ate quietly. They did not want to start an argument again because they did not want people in the offices below to hear them.

Sometimes people in the secret rooms had arguments.

Anne was the youngest person in the secret rooms. She always spoke the things in her head and did not always think first. This gave her many problems because other people did not always like this. But Anne's diary shows us many things. It shows us a funny and kind chatterbox. It also shows us a brave and happy girl. Life was difficult and dangerous, but Anne always smiled.

At a young age, Anne did not think about trees, flowers and birds. They were not very interesting for her. But life was different in the secret rooms, and her feelings changed. Now, Anne looked at the world through a window, and these things made her happy. She looked at the blue sky and saw birds flying past. She saw the green leaves and pretty flowers on the trees. These things became very important for Anne in the secret rooms, and she loved them.

Anne looked at the world through a window.

CHAPTER FIVE
Life in the secret rooms

In the day, many people worked in the offices below. The people in the secret rooms had to be very quiet and could not make any noise. They did not want anyone to hear them. This was very difficult for the group in the secret rooms. They could not have arguments. They had to find things to do, but these things had to be quiet. All the people in the secret rooms studied. Their helpers brought the group lessons and books to study.

LIFE IN THE SECRET ROOMS

**Anne and Margot learned new and
interesting things.**

In the secret rooms, Anne and Margot studied a lot. The sisters enjoyed learning new and interesting things, and they enjoyed reading, too. Everyone in the secret rooms loved reading and read a lot of books. Their helpers sometimes brought story books to the secret rooms. Everyone loved these "new books" days.

The group in the secret rooms got news about the war.

Everyone in the secret rooms wanted to know about the war. What was happening? Who was winning? Things often changed, and the group wanted to know about it. The helpers brought them food and other things, and they also told them the news. The group got news about their city and country, and about the world. They wanted to know everything.

LIFE IN THE SECRET ROOMS

The group had six helpers. These people knew Otto Frank from working with him. They were very angry about the war and very sad for Jewish people. They helped the people in the secret rooms as much as they could. But this was very dangerous for them. Many of the helpers had husbands or wives, and children. It was difficult for them to help the people in the secret rooms and help their own families, too. Anne understood this and wrote about it in her diary. She really wanted to thank them for helping her and her family.

Miep Gies Johannes Kleiman Victor Kugler

Bep Voskuijl Johannes Voskuijl Jan Gies

The helpers

Many people helped Jewish people in the war, but it was very dangerous for them. Sometimes, people told the Nazis about them, and the police took the helpers away. And, sometimes, the Nazis killed the helpers. But many people wanted to help. They did not want Hitler and the Nazis in their country, and they wanted to fight them. It was very difficult, but Jews needed these kind people. They were only able to hide because of their helpers.

Helping Jews was dangerous.

Sometimes, Anne and the group went down into the offices below and listened to the radio. Sometimes the radio gave them bad news, and sometimes it gave them good news. They wanted to know about the end of the war. They wanted to hear good news for the Allies and bad news for Hitler and the Nazis. They all thought a lot about the end of the war. Anne really wanted to go back to school. She wanted to have friends and be a normal young girl again.

Anne and her family wanted good news from the radio.

Anne could not bring Moortje to the secret rooms. She had to leave her cat at home. She was very sad about this, but there were two cats in the office building. Their names were Mouschi and Boche. Anne and Peter loved these cats and enjoyed playing with them.

Mouschi and Boche

BEANS

Sometimes the group in the secret rooms had arguments, but sometimes they were happy, too. They always tried to laugh and enjoy their time together. One day, Peter van Daan took some big bags of beans up to the top of the building. Suddenly, hundreds of beans rained down on Anne. She and Peter laughed and laughed, and later she wrote about it in her diary.

Hundreds of beans rained down on Anne.

Anne wrote in her diary about her life in the secret rooms. It was a difficult life, but life for Jews in the camps was much worse. Anne understood this and wrote about it in her diary. Life was not too bad for her. Some of the news on the radio was very bad. The Nazis were very cruel to millions of Jews. This made Anne sad, and she wrote about her feelings. But wars finish, and Anne always remembered this. She always had hope.

LIFE IN THE SECRET ROOMS

The eight people in the secret rooms were often frightened. Many people in Amsterdam had no food and no money, and they sometimes came into the office building at night. They looked for money and other things. This was dangerous for Anne and the group because the police often came after the people. The group had to be very quiet. They could not move or go to the toilet. They did not want the police to find them. This made the group very frightened.

The people in the secret rooms were frightened.

There were often bombings in Amsterdam.

The war made the city of Amsterdam very dangerous. There was a lot of fighting on the streets, and there were often bombings. The people in the secret rooms were often worried or frightened. At night, Anne did not like going down to the toilet. The secret rooms were quiet, and the noises from the city were strange. Anne worried a lot about her family and their friends.

But Anne's diary helped her a lot because she wrote about her feelings. She was often sad and frightened, but writing in her diary made her happy again.

Anne was in the secret rooms for two years. At the start, she was thirteen years old. Anne changed a lot in those two years.

LIFE IN THE SECRET ROOMS

On 28th March 1944, Anne listened to someone on the radio. They asked people to write diaries about the war and about the Nazis' control of the Netherlands. They wanted people to read these diaries after the war. Anne wanted people to read her diary, but she wanted to make it better first. She used her diary, but this time she wrote a story. She really wanted to become a famous writer after the war. Anne worked very hard on her "new diary", and in seventy-six days she wrote 200 pages. Anne wrote it in the secret rooms, and she also wrote a lot of other stories.

CHAPTER SIX
The Nazis find the secret rooms

In the early summer of 1944, there was some good news on the radio. The Allies were strong in their fight with Hitler and the Nazis. "The end of the war is coming," Anne thought. On 6th June 1944, the Allies invaded the north of France and fought the Nazis there. This gave the people in the secret rooms hope. The end of the war was close. Anne thought about school. She wanted to go back to her lessons and have a normal life again.

THE NAZIS FIND THE SECRET ROOMS

But then someone told the Nazis about the secret rooms and the Jewish people in them. On 4th August, the Nazis came and took the group of eight away. They also took two of their helpers. Then they sent them all to Nazi camps. They sent Otto, Edith, Anne and Margot to the Auschwitz-Birkenau camp in Poland. At the start, the three women were together. Sometimes, they were tired and hungry, but every day they had to work very hard.

The Nazis found the secret rooms.

Then, in October 1944, the Nazis moved Anne and Margot to Bergen-Belsen camp in Germany. Edith was very worried. "Where are my daughters?" she asked the Nazis. But they did not tell her. Edith became more and more worried and got very thin. She then became ill, and, in January 1945, she sadly died.

Anne and Margot went to Bergen-Belsen camp in Germany.

THE NAZIS FIND THE SECRET ROOMS

Anne and Margot became ill, too, in early 1945. Many people became ill in the Nazi camps. The camps were very dirty, and people were hungry and tired. They did not have very much to eat, and they had to work very hard. Sadly, Margot and Anne died in the Bergen-Belsen camp. Margot was only nineteen, and Anne was fifteen.

Seven of the people from the secret rooms died in Nazi camps before the end of the war. Only Otto Frank saw the Allies win.

CHAPTER SEVEN
Anne's diary

Otto Frank came out of Auschwitz-Birkenau camp on 27th January 1945. The Allies came to Auschwitz, and the Jewish people in the camp could go home. Otto went back to Amsterdam. In Amsterdam, his friends told him about Margot and Anne, and one of their helpers gave him Anne's diary. She found it in the secret rooms. She really wanted to give it to Anne after the war, but she could not. Otto read Anne's diary and understood her feelings. His daughter was a kind and wonderful young woman.

A helper gave Anne's diary to Otto.

Otto loved Anne's diary. Her writing was interesting and intelligent, but it was also important. Otto showed the diary to a lot of people. He showed it to people in the Frank family and to his friends. They all loved Anne's diary, too. It was important because it showed the truth of life for Jewish people in the war. Hiding from the Nazis was difficult and dangerous, and people were very frightened. Anne was also a funny and wonderful young girl living in a strange world. Her writing shows this, and people love reading it.

Anne wanted to become a famous writer. Otto wanted Anne to become a famous writer, too. He wanted people across the world to read her diary. He worked very hard to make this true, and his daughter is now one of the most famous writers in the world.

Otto found a small business, and the business made Anne's diary into a book. In 1947, they made 3,000 books, and people quickly bought them. They had to make more books only six months later. In 1952, a business called Doubleday told the story of Anne's diary in the English language. Today, you can buy Anne's diary in more than seventy different languages.

People can visit the secret rooms.

In 1960, the office building and the secret rooms opened for people to visit. The secret rooms help people to understand Anne's writing. Today, thousands of people visit the secret rooms and see Anne's bedroom and her pictures on the walls.

Anne's diary helps us to understand the life of Jewish people in the Second World War. Hitler and the Nazis took control of many countries and were very cruel to the Jews there. People read Anne's diary and say, "It must never happen again."

TIMELINE

1929
Anne Frank comes into the world on 12th June in Frankfurt am Main, Germany.

1933
Adolf Hitler and the Nazis take control of Germany. Anne Frank's family leave Germany because people are cruel to Jews.

1934
The Frank family go to Amsterdam in the Netherlands.

1942

Margot Frank gets a letter from the Nazi government about a work camp. The Franks, the van Daans and Mr Dussel hide from the Nazis in the secret rooms.

1939

The Second World War starts on 1st September.

1940

The Nazis invade the Netherlands.

Margot Frank
Pr.ᴄᴄ-ˡᵈ.ʒ- 48
1155 Amsterdam

JEW

1942-1944
The Frank family hide from the Nazis and Anne writes her diary.

1944
The Nazis come to the secret rooms. They send the eight people to different camps.

1945
Margot and Anne become ill and die. The Allies win the war in Europe on 8th May.

1952
Doubleday makes a book of Anne's diary in English.

1947
Otto Frank makes Anne's diary into a book.

1960
People start to visit the office building and the secret rooms.

During-reading questions

CHAPTER ONE

1 Who did Anne Frank and her family hide from?
2 Where did Anne and her family hide?
3 Anne died at a young age. How old was she?
4 How many people hid in the secret rooms?
5 Why is Anne's diary important?

CHAPTER TWO

1 When did Adolf Hitler and the Nazis take control of Germany?
2 Why did Anne and her family go to Amsterdam in the Netherlands?
3 What started on 1st September 1939?
4 How many Jews did the Nazis kill in the war?

CHAPTER THREE

1 What language did Anne and Margot learn?
2 Anne's diary was her best friend. What name did she give it?
3 When did the Nazis invade the Netherlands? Did life change for Jewish people?
4 Anne's mother and father made a plan. Why? What was it?

CHAPTER FOUR

1 What did Margot get on 5th July 1942? What was it about?
2 Anne and her family hid in the secret rooms. Where were the secret rooms?
3 Why did the people in the secret rooms have to be very quiet?
4 How did the people in the secret rooms get food?
5 What things became important for Anne in the secret rooms?

CHAPTER FIVE

1 Which days did everyone in the secret rooms love?
2 Why was life dangerous for the helpers?
3 Why were the people in the secret rooms often frightened?
4 What did Anne want to become after the war?

CHAPTER SIX

1 Who came to the secret rooms on 4th August 1944?
2 Where did the Nazis send Otto, Edith, Anne and Margot?
3 How many of the eight people from the secret rooms died in Nazi camps?

CHAPTER SEVEN

1 Who gave Anne's diary to Otto?
2 What did Otto do with Anne's diary?
3 In 1960, what opened for people to visit?

After-reading questions

1 How was life bad for Jewish people in the Second World War?

2 How was life for the people in the secret rooms, do you think?

3 How was life for the Franks' helpers, do you think?

4 What kind of girl was Anne?

5 What do you think about Anne's story? How do people today think about the Second World War because of her diary?

Exercises

CHAPTER ONE

1) **Match the words with their definitions in your notebook.**

Example: 1 – f

1 life
2 become
3 brave
4 secret
5 feelings
6 interesting
7 dangerous
8 cruel

a not kind
b a thing or person that you want to know more about
c when something can hurt you
d to start to be something
e Only some people know about this thing.
f from the start of living to the end of living
g happiness, sadness, anger or fear, for example
h when a person is not frightened

CHAPTER TWO

2) **Write the correct adjectives in your notebook.**
1 Anne had an *older* / **oldest** sister called Margot.
2 In Nazi Germany, life became very **interesting** / **difficult** for Jewish people.
3 "German people are **better** / **more good** than Jewish people," the Nazis said.
4 "German people are **more important** / **most important** than Jewish people," the Nazis said.
5 Nazi Germany was too **expensive** / **dangerous** for Anne and her family.
6 For six years, Anne and her family were **happy** / **brave** in Amsterdam.

CHAPTER THREE

3 **Are these sentences *true* or *false*? Write the correct answers in your notebook.**

In 1940, life changed for Jewish people in Amsterdam:

1 Jews had to wear a green star. ....*false*..........
2 Jews could not have a bicycle.
3 Jews could not use trams, but they could travel in cars.
4 Jews could go shopping between 9 a.m. and 5 p.m.
5 Jews could not go out of their homes between 8 p.m. and 6 a.m.
6 Jews could go to the cinema on Tuesdays.

CHAPTER FOUR

4 **Complete these sentences in your notebook with the past simple form of the verbs.**

1 Anne ....*wrote*.......... (**write**) about her parents in her diary.
2 Anne's teacher .... (**tell**) her to write a story about a chatterbox.
3 Many Jewish people .... (**have to**) work in Nazi camps.
4 The Franks .... (**build**) a bookcase over the door to the secret rooms.
5 The people in the secret rooms .... (**can**) only open a window at night.
6 The Frank family .... (**buy**) their food on the black market.
7 Life was difficult in the secret rooms, but Anne always .... (**smile**).

CHAPTER FIVE

5 Complete these sentences in your notebook, using the nouns from the box.

war	school	radio	arguments
	writer	camps	helpers

1 Everyone in the secret rooms wanted to know about the ......*war*.........
2 The Franks' .... were angry about the war and sad for Jewish people.
3 Anne wanted to go back to .... after the war.
4 Sometimes the people in the secret rooms had ...., but sometimes they were happy.
5 Life was difficult, but life for Jews in the .... was much worse.
6 Some of the news on the .... was very bad.
7 Anne wanted to be a famous ....

CHAPTER SIX

6 Look at the picture on page 45, and answer the questions in your notebook.
1 Who is this?
2 When is this?
3 What is he doing?
4 Where did they send the people from the secret rooms?

CHAPTER SEVEN

7 Make these sentences positive in your notebook.

1 After the Auschwitz-Birkenau camp, Otto Frank didn't go back to Amsterdam.

   After the Auschwitz-Birkenau camp, Otto Frank went back to Amsterdam.

2 Otto didn't show Anne's diary to a lot of people.
3 Anne's diary doesn't tell us about the life of Jewish people in the war.
4 In the war, hiding from the Nazis wasn't difficult.
5 Today, you can't buy Anne's diary in lots of different languages.

ALL CHAPTERS

8 Match the words to the pictures in your notebook.
Example: 1 – b

1 hide   a

2 diary   b

3 win   c

4 exam   d

Project work

1 Anne Frank lived in the Second World War. Look online, and find out about the Second World War in your country. Find out about these things:
   a Did your country fight in the war?
   b Did your country fight with Germany or the Allies?
   c Was life good or bad in your country in the war? Why?
   d Did your country change after the war?

2 Anne Frank was born in Frankfurt in Germany. Find out more about the city, and make a poster. Draw some pictures for your poster.

3 Today, people can visit the office building and the secret rooms in Amsterdam. Look online, and find out about the secret rooms. Make an information leaflet.

4 Imagine you are Anne Frank. Think about your time in the secret rooms. Complete the table with the good things and the bad things about living in the secret rooms

Good things about the secret room	Bad things about the secret room

An answer key for all questions and exercises can be found at **www.penguinreaders.co.uk**

Glossary

become (v.)
past tense: **became**
to start to be something

black market (n.)
People buy and sell things on the *black market* because it is difficult to buy them in shops. Buying and selling things on the *black market* is against the law (= the things people can and cannot do in their country).

brave (adj.)
A *brave* person is not frightened.

business (n.)
A *business* buys and sells things.

camp (n.)
a place with buildings. In the *Second World War*, some people had to live and work in *camps*, and they could not leave them.

control (n. and v.)
You *invade* a place and take *control* of it. People live in that place, and you *control* them, too. You tell them to do things, and they must do them.

cruel (adj.)
not kind

dangerous (adj.)
Something can hurt you. It is *dangerous* for you.

feelings (n.)
Sometimes, you are happy, sad, angry or frightened, for example. "*Feeling*" is the noun of "feel".

government (n.)
a group of important people. They say what must happen in a country.

ill (adj.)
An *ill* person is not very well.

interesting (adj.)
You want to know more about an *interesting* thing or person.

invade (v.)
to go into another country and take *control* of it

Jew (n.); **Jewish** (adj.)
The *Jews* are a group of people. *Millions* of *Jews* died in the *Second World War*. After this, many of them left Europe to live in Israel. *Jewish* is the adjective of *Jew*.

life (n.)
1. from the start of living, to the end of living. This is a person's *life*.
2. how a person lives. There are a lot of problems in a difficult *life*.

million (n.)
the number 1,000,000

Nazi (n.)
The *Nazis* were Germany's *government* in the *Second World War*. Adolf Hitler *controlled* the *Nazis*.

rule (n.)
You must or must not do some things. These are the *rules*.

Second World War (n.)
a war (= fighting between countries or groups of people) in Europe, Africa and Asia between 1939 and 1945

secret (adj.)
Only some people know about a *secret* thing.

worry (v.)
You are not happy because maybe something bad will happen. You are *worrying* about something.